Everything
You Need to
Know About

Chicken
Pox and
Shingles

Regular visits to the doctor can help you maintain good health.

Everything You Need to Know About Chicken Pox and Shingles

Jennifer Plum

The Rosen Publishing Group, Inc.
New York

This book is dedicated to my mom, Lillian.

Published in 2001 by The Rosen Publishing Group, Inc.
29 East 21st Street, New York, NY 10010

Library of Congress Cataloging-in-Publication Data

Plum, Jennifer.
    Everything you need to know about chicken pox and shingles/Jennifer Plum.—1st ed.
    p. cm. -- (Need to know library)
Includes bibliographical references and index.
ISBN 0-8239-3323-7 (alk. paper)
1. Chicken pox—Juvenile literature. 2. Shingles (Disease)—Juvenile literature. [1. Chicken pox. 2. Shingles (Disease) 3. Diseases.] I. Title. II. Series.
RC125 .P58 2000
616.9'14—dc21
                                    00-010631

Manufactured in the United States of America

Contents

Introduction

Marcus came home from school feeling sleepy and cranky. His dad suggested that he take a nap before dinner, but when dinnertime came he still didn't feel well. He had no appetite at all. The next morning, his brother woke up him for school but Marcus didn't think he was well enough to go. He was still tired and now he felt feverish, too. Marcus's dad took his temperature, and sure enough it was 101. By the end of the day, there were two red bumps on his stomach that were starting to itch. It certainly looked like it was chicken pox, especially when the bumps kept on itching like crazy. Marcus spent the next few days trying not to itch and scratch the red rash that by now was covering most of his body.

◆　　　◆　　　◆

It was Tuesday and Lucinda was looking forward to the weekend because she would get to see her grandchildren at the family barbecue. However, she had not been feeling well since the morning. She went outside to her garden, but after only one hour, she had to go in to rest. In the evening, she felt a band of pain stretching across the middle of her back. She wondered if she had pulled a muscle while weeding. After dinner, Lucinda's friend Esther called, and when Lucinda described the shooting pain that she was feeling, Esther told her to check if there was a rash forming on her back, and suggested that she might have shingles. Esther's guess was right—Lucinda did have a rash on her back. She saw it in the mirror. Lucinda called her doctor to find out more about shingles, wondering if she did have it and if that was why she felt so rotten.

Even though both Lucinda and Marcus were suffering from different symptoms, they had one thing in common—a rash. Both shingles and chicken pox are caused by the varicella-zoster virus, or VZV. Although the same virus is responsible for both illnesses, it produces different results in the body. Chicken pox, which is more common among children, causes an itchy rash and flulike symptoms. Once the VZV virus is in the body, it never leaves; it stays in the nerve cells and may wake up years later, causing shingles. While chicken pox affects mostly children, shingles affects mostly elderly people. Another major difference between the two diseases is that while the defining feature of chicken pox is that it is very itchy, the most common complaint from shingles sufferers is the pain that they feel. However, both diseases are painful.

Chicken pox and shingles are extremely common, and medical technology is being used to explore ways to stop these diseases from continually affecting our lives. In this book we will identify and discuss the symptoms of both diseases. We will also explore and learn more about what is being done to protect us from falling victim to chicken pox and shingles. And lastly, we will discuss what we can do to help those who are suffering from either chicken pox or shingles.

Chapter One

What Is Chicken Pox?

Chicken pox is a viral disease that is highly contagious, meaning that it can be easily passed from one person to another. You may remember staying home from school when you were younger and being covered with itchy red blisters. That was chicken pox. The chicken pox virus, more formally known as varicella-zoster, is a very common childhood disease. The National Institute of Allergy and Infectious Diseases (NIAID) estimates that close to four million people are infected with chicken pox each year.

The Cause of Chicken Pox

As previously mentioned, a virus called varicella-zoster, or VZV, causes chicken pox. This virus is a part of the herpesvirus family. One member of this family, the herpes simplex virus (HSV), is often associated with the sexually transmitted disease known as herpes, and with the common cold sore. The herpes virus typically causes inflammation of the skin or blisters. The chicken pox virus (VZV) is similar to herpes simplex in that once the virus infects the body, it remains there for good. This means that the chicken pox virus can hide out in nerve cells and be reactivated later in life. This is what happens when a person gets shingles, which will be discussed further in chapter 3.

The Making of a Virus

Viruses cause infectious diseases, ranging from the common cold to rabies or AIDS. A virus is a very simple structure, but it can cause many problems in the human body. Viruses are very dangerous for people who have a weakened immune system. Your immune system is your body's natural defense against infections and bacteria.

A virus (such as the VZV virus) consists of many small particles. A virus is made up of two parts—a genetic material, such as DNA or RNA, and protein. The protein coat makes up the outer shell of the virus, which protects the genetic material. Inside the shell is the DNA or RNA, which contain instructions for making more viruses.

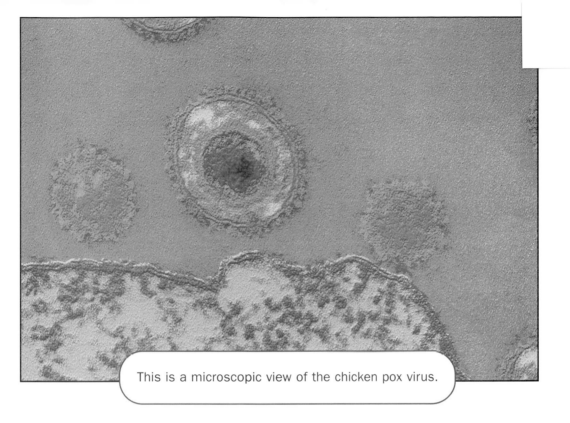

This is a microscopic view of the chicken pox virus.

A virus is not alive until it gets into a living cell where it is able to reproduce. The living cell then becomes the host for the virus. A virus attacks a single cell. It will attach itself to the cell membrane and make a hole in the cell wall. Through this hole, the virus will send its own DNA or RNA code. Once this happens, the DNA or RNA of the virus can take over the healthy cell by copying itself. The virus will make copies of itself until the cell is filled to capacity and bursts open. This allows the virus to spread through the body.

Varicella-Zoster (VZV)

The chicken pox virus, or VZV, will first attack the lining of the nose and the mouth. The makeup of VZV is

Since the chicken pox virus is easily spread among children, it is a particular danger in school classrooms and day care facilities.

more complicated than the average virus; the protein covering of the virus contains finger-like projections that attach themselves to the fragile cells in the lining of the nose and mouth. As the virus multiplies in the nose and mouth, it will soon move on to the skin cells. This produces the itchy red rash that is characteristic of chicken pox. Finally, some virus particles may settle into the nerve cells. Here the virus may remain inactive for many years. It may resurface later, however, and produce shingles.

How Does Chicken Pox Spread?

Chicken pox is very contagious and spreads quickly through a classroom, play group, day care center, or family. Once one student in a class or one guest at a birthday party comes down with chicken pox, it is likely that most of the other children have already been affected. When one child in a family contracts chicken pox, there is a ninety percent chance that siblings or a parent will become sick, too. As the virus moves through a family, the children who are infected by the disease later often suffer more serious symptoms. There is no explanation for this.

The chicken pox virus is an airborne virus—this means that it is carried in the air when an infected person coughs or sneezes. It can also be spread through the discharge from the skin rash of a person who is sick. In rare cases, a person who is suffering from shingles can pass the VZV virus along to an unexposed person. In this case, the infected person would come down with chicken pox, not shingles.

Once the body has been exposed to the virus, it takes time before symptoms begin to show. The infected person will not feel sick for some time. This time before any symptoms appear is called the incubation period. The incubation period for chicken pox can be anywhere from ten to twenty-one days.

During the incubation period, the virus is multiplying in the body. However, an infected person will have no idea that he or she is sick. This makes it very easy for chicken pox to spread from person to person. It is possible to spend time with a friend who is not aware that he or she is carrying the chicken pox virus. By the time the friend starts showing symptoms, it is too late to avoid catching VZV from him or her. Chances are that the person already has caught chicken pox.

A Rite of Passage

Although it is possible for anyone to contract chicken pox, this virus most often affects children. It is like a rite of passage for many—an event associated closely with the normal experience of childhood. Most parents assume that their children will not get through adolescence without having had chicken pox.

A child may be infected with the VZV virus and not even know it, because he or she feels fine.

Of the estimated four million people who are infected with VZV annually, 90 percent are children under the age of fifteen. Chicken pox occurs most frequently in those children between the ages of two and ten. Chicken pox is usually a mild virus and is more irritating than dangerous for most people. The virus causes a fever and an itchy rash made up of pus-filled blisters. There are few long-term health risks for most children who catch chicken pox at an early age.

If you are not infected with the varicella-zoster virus as a child, you become susceptible to catching a more serious strain of the virus as an adult. Chicken pox causes approximately fifty to one hundred deaths each year, according to Merck Laboratories medical research. However, an adult with chicken pox is ten times more likely to require a trip to the hospital, and twenty times more likely to die due to complications.

Chapter Two | Symptoms and Treatment

*C*hristina could not wait for her class trip to the new rainforest exhibit at the zoo. She loved learning about different animals and was excited about the big trip on Friday. However, when Christina woke up on Monday morning she was not feeling well. Her mom was worried because she was not herself; instead, she was cranky and tired. Christina's mom remembered that a boy who was at a birthday party with Christina two weeks earlier had come down with chicken pox. Mrs. Mosely decided to keep Christina home from school.

By afternoon, Christina was flushed and had a fever. By the next morning, her mom's concerns were proved true: She found two red spots—one on Christina's back and one near her ankle. These

The first signs of the chicken pox are usually fatigue and fever. An itchy, red rash typically follows.

two spots multiplied and Christina spent the next few days in bed covered with itchy blisters as the rash spread over her body. She was too tired to play and was not hungry, even for lasagna, her favorite food. She struggled not to scratch at the blisters, and her mom prepared warm oatmeal baths to relieve the itching. Christina missed out on her class trip, but her dad promised that he would take her to the zoo when she was feeling better. Christina had more energy in a few days and slowly her scabs healed and faded.

The symptoms of chicken pox are often obvious, especially if you are aware that you or your child has been exposed to the virus. Christina's mom had an idea that her daughter might come down with chicken pox after finding out that a friend had become sick two weeks earlier. All of the children at that birthday party had been exposed to the virus. For some, it was just a matter of time before they were home from school with chicken pox.

The Symptoms of Chicken Pox

Symptoms of chicken pox can appear anywhere between ten to twenty-one days after someone has been exposed to the varicella-zoster virus. The most common indicator of chicken pox is the itchy red rash, but other symptoms will appear generally two days earlier. These include:

- Achiness
- Tiredness
- Irritability
- Fever
- Sore throat
- Swollen glands
- Loss of appetite
- Joint pain

The itchy, red blisters that make up chicken pox often are seen first on the back, chest, and scalp. From there they may spread to the arms, legs, and face. They can spread to anywhere on the body, including the eyelids, armpits, and even internally, like inside the mouth. It is possible for some people to develop anywhere from 150 blisters (in an average case of chicken pox) to 250–500 blisters (in an extreme case).

The Rash

Each pox, or lesion, goes through the same process. It starts as a flat, red area that will soon rise off the skin to form a bump. This is known as a papule. Next, the papule will begin to look more like a blister as a cloudy substance (known as pus) is created inside. At this stage, the lesion is called a pustule. Finally, the pustule will form a dry hard covering, similar to the scabs that you get when a cut is healing.

Can you guess how long this whole process takes? Though it sounds like it would take a long time, it only takes the body a few hours to go through all of these steps. As the red bumps go through the process of change, new ones are constantly forming. So it is possible for an infected person to have the pox in many different stages at the same time.

No Scratching Allowed!

The biggest concern for caretakers of a person with chicken pox is to keep the infected person from scratching the rash. As you can see in the process of the pox, the pustule is filled with pus, which contains the virus.

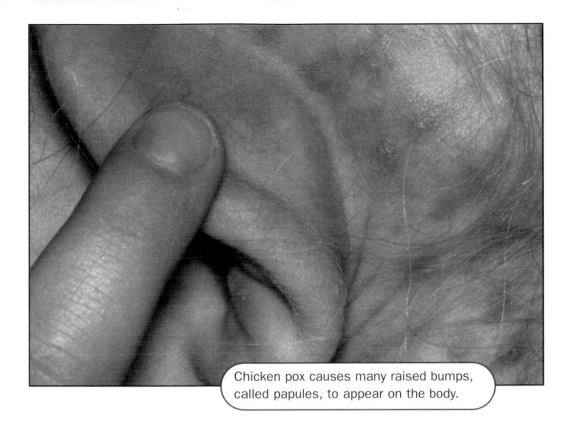

Chicken pox causes many raised bumps, called papules, to appear on the body.

When the pustules are scratched, this pus is released from the blister and can spread across the body.

As you know when you get a cut or scrape on your body, a scab forms. This hard covering protects the broken skin from germs. It also allows the delicate tissue to heal underneath while it prevents infection. If this scab is broken, bacteria from underneath fingernails and on hands can get into the wound. This may cause an infection of the pustule. And an infection can lead to permanent scarring of the skin.

Going to the Doctor

Did you notice that Christina never went to the doctor when she had chicken pox? This might seem strange,

Because of the danger of contagion, doctors often recommend that kids with chicken pox not come to the office.

as most people first visit a doctor for a diagnosis. However, with chicken pox, a parent or guardian can easily make a diagnosis at home.

Because chicken pox is so contagious, doctors would rather treat a patient over the phone. If an infected child is brought to the waiting room, the virus can spread to a whole new group of people. It is only necessary to make a visit to the doctor's office if there are complications from chicken pox. A complication might be a high fever that lasts for a long time or a painful and infected rash. But in most instances, a case of chicken pox is one time when a trip to the doctor is probably not necessary. The virus needs to run its course and soon the infected person should start feeling better.

Is There Medication That Will Help?

In the same way that a trip to the doctor is not necessary with a normal case of chicken pox, there is generally no need for special medicine. People have developed many home remedies to make chicken pox less upsetting and itchy. In the past there was no prescription or over-the-counter medicine for chicken pox. In 1992, the FDA (the Food and Drug Administration) approved treatment using a drug called Zovirax.

Zovirax, or acyclovir, is an antiviral drug. This means that it will attack the varicella-zoster virus that is invading the body. After the first red bumps appear, the more quickly the treatment begins, the fewer sores will be created. The treatment can also shorten the length of time that the rash develops and spreads in the body. It is not a cure for chicken pox, but it does relieve some symptoms.

This drug is only necessary in high-risk or severe cases. It is recommended for those who are especially sensitive to the virus, including premature babies, teenagers, adults, and those with weakened immune systems. Despite benefits, Zorivax can be expensive and inconvenient. It is not the answer for everyone.

Home Remedies

While medication is not necessary, people develop many different home remedies to help ease the discomfort of chicken pox. The first rule of home remedies for chicken pox is to remember that cool water is more helpful than hot water. A cool bath can help lower a fever and provide a soothing break from itching. However, a hot bath raises the body temperature and only causes more itching. Some people find that soaking in a bath of uncooked oatmeal, baking soda, or cornstarch reduces the itching. Another way to relieve itching is to apply calamine lotion to the pustules.

There are some over-the-counter medicines that can be used to reduce pain and fever. Fever can be lowered by acetaminophen, which is found in Tylenol. Also, an infected person may find relief by taking an antihistamine to reduce the inflammation and itching.

Never Take Aspirin If You Have Chicken Pox!

It is extremely important to remember that a person infected with chicken pox should never take aspirin for relief. Aspirin may cause Reye's syndrome, which will be discussed later in this book. More information about the relationship between chicken pox and aspirin will be discussed in chapter 4.

Good Hygiene and Other Necessary Precautions

Doctors suggest that fingernails be clipped short and hands kept clean so that scratching is less harsh. It may also help for a child to wear gloves or socks on

Home remedies, such as a bath of uncooked oatmeal, baking soda, or cornstarch, can help soothe the itching of chicken pox.

his or her hands, especially when sleeping at night. It is important that young children understand that they should not scratch at the rash regardless of how uncomfortable they may feel. Later in life when they are scar-free, they will be happy that they followed this simple, but very difficult, rule.

Can I Catch It Again?

It is a relief to know that once you have chicken pox you will probably not experience it again. However, even if you have had chicken pox you can still get sick from the varicella-zoster virus. Remember how VZV hides out in nerve cells as it makes its way through the body? These cells can resurface later in life to cause the painful disease of shingles. Shingles will be discussed more fully in chapter 3.

Chapter Three

What Is Shingles?

Do you remember learning how the virus that causes chicken pox—the varicella-zoster virus, or VZV—can hide out in the nerve cells? This virus may be inactive, or asleep, in the nerve cells for years. It never dies, even after chicken pox is gone. You might never know that it was there at all—that is, unless it wakes up and causes shingles.

How Is Shingles Different from Chicken Pox?

Shingles is a member of the herpesvirus family just like chicken pox. It is also called herpes zoster. Many of the symptoms are similar to chicken pox. However, shingles is often more painful than the common childhood disease. The skin rash that comes with shingles is similar to that caused by chicken pox; but as opposed to chicken pox, where the rash can cover most parts of the body, the rash caused by shingles attacks a small area of the body. And instead of the itchiness that comes with the pox, the shingles rash causes pain.

Who Is at Risk of Getting Shingles?

You may be wondering why some people who have had the chicken pox virus get shingles while others never do. People who have had chicken pox are at a higher risk of getting shingles. The VZV Research Foundation states that one in seven individuals may have a reappearance of the VZV virus as shingles before they reach eighty-five years of age. However, the disease can strike anyone, though it is most commonly found in individuals over the age of fifty.

Weakened Immune System

People with a weakened immune system are at the greatest risk of contracting shingles. As we learned earlier, your immune system is your body's natural defense against infections and bacteria. Sometimes the immune system gets run down, which prevents it from

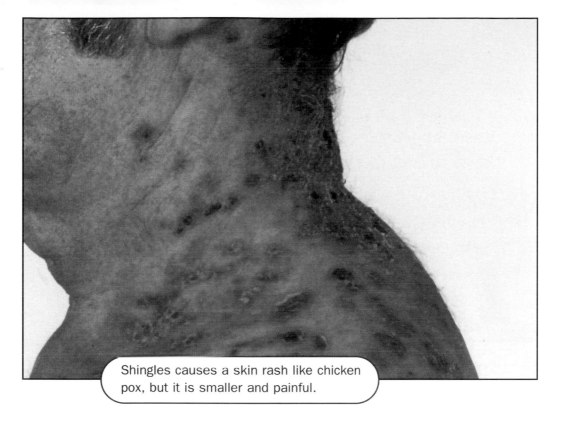

Shingles causes a skin rash like chicken pox, but it is smaller and painful.

fighting all foreign substances effectively. Certain medical treatments, such as chemotherapy or radiation treatment, that are used to treat cancer patients, weaken the immune system and leave an individual open to contract shingles. Other people who are at risk are those with HIV, leukemia, or AIDS, and those undergoing organ transplant operations.

Stress

Recent studies suggest that stress may be a trigger for shingles. Stress can be caused by a physical change in the body, such as exposure to either very hot or very cold weather. Stress is also caused by a strain on one's emotions, including constant feelings of anger and fear. Unfortunately, there are many cases of shingles in healthy people for which their doctors have no explanation.

Aging

The elderly are more likely to get shingles because the immune system naturally weakens with age. Once infected, it is more difficult for an elderly person to recover quickly from shingles. The older a person is, the more serious the case of shingles.

Diagnosing the Pain

A rash is one symptom that chicken pox and shingles have in common. The difference is that with shingles, the rash is concentrated in the area where the nerve is being attacked, as opposed to the widespread rash of chicken pox. Also, the shingles rash causes a burning, painful sensation instead of an itchy, uncomfortable rash like chicken pox.

The shingles rash, more contained than that of chicken pox and affecting only one area of the body, appears as a trail of blisters on the skin. This trail mirrors the path that the virus is following inside the body. In the case of shingles, the VZV virus attacks the nerves, so the rash appears along a nerve path. Shingles usually appear on the stomach, back, or face.

Unlike chicken pox, the shingles rash concentrates in the skin above the infected nerve cell.

Possible First Symptoms of Shingles

The first symptoms of shingles may come before the rash does. Some of these include:

- Burning pain or itching on one side of the body
- Numbness or a tingling feeling in a particular region of the body
- Chills
- Fever
- Upset stomach
- Headache

Many of the symptoms of shingles can be mistaken for another sickness. However, the pain occurring on just one side of the body is usually the giveaway that the infection is shingles. It is possible to have shingles without the rash. In this case, the symptoms are all the same except for the absence of blisters. This very rare type of shingles is called zoster sine herpes.

What Happens Next?

After the first warning signals of regular shingles appear, the rash begins to form. This can happen anywhere from one to fourteen days after the first symptom is noticed. After about two to four days, the blisters will fill with fluid. Then it will be another two to four weeks before these pustules will crust over and form scabs. Even after the blisters heal, it is likely that the pain will remain. If the pain continues for an unusually long period of time, it is likely that the patient has developed PHN, or post-herpetic neuralgia. This will be discussed further in chapter 4.

Is Shingles Contagious?

Knowing that chicken pox is so contagious, you might assume that the same is true for shingles. Determining who is vulnerable around someone with shingles can be a little confusing. You cannot catch shingles from anyone—the infection comes from within the body. A person with shingles cannot give shingles to someone else. Nor can a person catch the VZV virus in the form of shingles from someone who has chicken pox.

However, a person who has never been exposed to the VZV virus can catch chicken pox from someone who has shingles. For example, imagine that your grandfather or an older friend has shingles. If you have never had chicken pox, you could catch the VZV virus from them. You will not contract the shingles rash, but the VZV virus will cause a chicken pox infection in your body.

Treatment for Shingles If It Is Diagnosed on Time

The good news about shingles is that there are treatments to reduce the pain. However, in order for the treatment to be effective, the doctor must diagnose shingles within seventy-two hours of the start of the infection. There is a prescription drug available called acyclovir that is helpful. This drug is a member of the antiviral drug family. This is the same medicine used to treat severe cases of chicken pox. This medicine can shorten the course of the sickness and speed up the recovery process.

Treatment If Shingles Is Not Diagnosed Within Seventy-Two Hours

If shingles is not diagnosed within seventy-two hours (which it often is not), then there are some

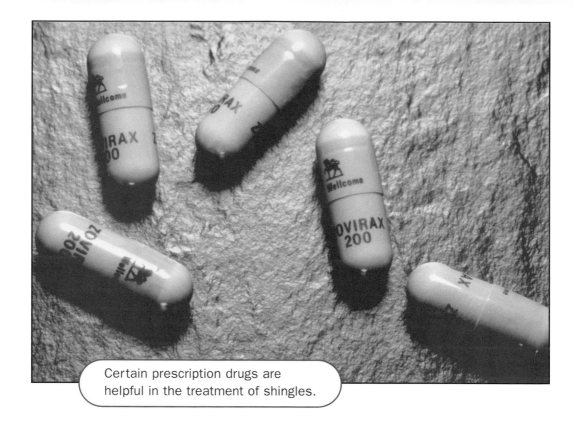

Certain prescription drugs are
helpful in the treatment of shingles.

other remedies available to make shingles less
painful. Doctors may recommend that you take over-
the-counter painkillers or sedatives to reduce pain
and itching. Home remedies such as a cold compress
or antibacterial lotion may help to reduce the pain of
the rash.

Can You Catch Shingles Again?

Another big difference between chicken pox and
shingles is that you can catch shingles again. Unlike
chicken pox, you do not develop immunity to that
strain of the VZV virus after having shingles once.
According to the VZV Foundation, one out of every

five patients gets shingles again. The virus will not attack the same nerve cells twice. This means that if someone does get shingles more than once, the rash will appear on a different part of the body. Recent studies show that it is not the same shingles virus that reappears again, but a similar herpes virus.

Chapter Four

Complications

Jeff's older brother Anthony had chicken pox first, so no one was shocked when Jeff started complaining about feeling very tired. Anthony had come down with chicken pox after it spread through his soccer team. He was in bed for three days, but once the scabs started forming he was feeling much better. His mom didn't even have a hard time stopping him from scratching!

But two weeks later when Jeff came down with chicken pox, it was obvious that there was something wrong. His rash was oozing and infected. Jeff's fever was climbing higher—when it hit 104 degrees his mom took him to the doctor. She knew that she could not give him aspirin, and the over-the-counter Tylenol was not helping his symptoms.

The doctor said that Jeff had a staph infection, which happens when staphylococcus bacteria enter the body through an opening in the skin. The doctor pointed out that this was common in children under five who have chicken pox. He prescribed an antibiotic to stop the infection from spreading. Within a few days, Jeff was feeling a little bit better. And after a few weeks he was back in school.

Who Is at Risk of a More Serious Case of Chicken Pox?

In most healthy people, chicken pox is only a nuisance. However, some people are more prone to side effects related to chicken pox. For these people, an encounter with the varicella-zoster virus can mean serious damage to the body. Some people who are at risk for complicated chicken pox are:

+ Newborns

+ Adolescents

+ Adults

+ Pregnant women

+ People with weakened immune systems, including those with HIV, AIDS, or leukemia

Why Is Chicken Pox More Serious in Adults?

According to the National Coalition for Adult Immunization, less than 5 percent of adults are likely to develop chicken pox. However, adults are twenty-five times more likely to die from chicken pox than are children. When adults catch chicken pox it is also likely that they will be hospitalized for conditions such as pneumonia, bacterial infections, and high fevers. It is recommended that adults who have never been infected with VZV receive immunizations against this virus. This will be discussed further in chapter 5.

Chicken Pox and Pregnancy

Chicken pox can be dangerous during pregnancy. A mother helps to create her unborn child's immune system by passing down antibodies to certain viruses. Therefore, a pregnant woman who has had chicken pox before and has developed immunity to the VZV virus will pass this along to her baby. These antibodies can protect the baby for the first three months of his or her life.

If a pregnant woman who has never had chicken pox is exposed to the virus, she should tell her doctor. If she were to develop chicken pox anywhere from five days to forty-eight hours before she delivers the baby, the newborn might be born with the rash. This could cause complications for the mother and especially for

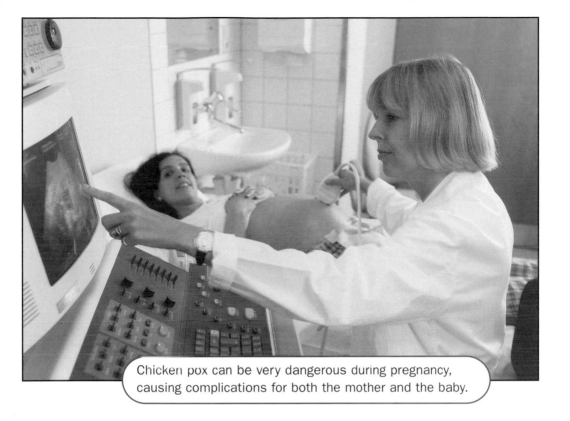

Chicken pox can be very dangerous during pregnancy, causing complications for both the mother and the baby.

the baby, who has few defenses to sickness. Exposure of the fetus to the chicken pox virus during the first twenty weeks of pregnancy may cause birth defects such as retardation or malformed bones. Such defects occur rarely, however.

Chicken Pox and a Weakened Immune System

As you learned earlier, your immune system protects you from getting sick. Some people who have been sick for a long time or who take special medications may have weakened immune systems. Diseases such as AIDS or leukemia that weaken the immune system make someone more prone to catching a serious case of chicken pox. Taking steroids also weakens the human immune system and makes one more vulnerable when fighting chicken pox. This puts asthma patients who are treated with steroids at risk. Finally, people who have had organ transplants are at risk of complicated chicken pox. This is because before receiving a transplant, people are given drugs that weaken the immune system. This is done so that the body will not reject the organ, thinking that it is a dangerous foreign substance.

Unusual Circumstances

Chicken pox is a common disease. While uncomfortable, it is rarely dangerous. However, there are times when this common infection requires a trip to the doctor. Health professionals recommend that you contact a doctor if you experience strange symptoms beyond the expected rash, low fever, and low energy. Some of the warning signals of problematic chicken pox include:

- A fever higher than 103 degrees
- Dizzy spells
- Rapid or irregular heartbeat
- Vomiting
- Loss of muscle coordination/body tremors
- Stiff neck
- Infected blisters

Sometimes all it takes is a prescription for a bacterial infection to feel better. Like in the story about Jeff at the beginning of this chapter, sores may become infected with the staphylococcus bacteria. It is also possible for the rash to become infected with the streptococcus bacteria. This is the same bacteria that causes strep throat when it attacks the respiratory system. While these infections make the sickness last longer and feel more uncomfortable, they can easily be treated with antibiotics. Once treated, the only negative side effect of most such infections is scarring where the infected rash was scratched.

Effects on the Nervous System and Respiratory System

Chicken pox complications related to the nervous system are rare, but can be very serious. In very few cases, the VZV virus can cause a swelling of the brain, known as encephalitis. While this is most common in children aged five to fourteen, it is life-threatening for adults. This inflammation usually lasts two weeks and can result in possible hearing loss, convulsions, coma, paralysis of the body, or brain damage including retardation, learning disabilities, and hyperactivity disorders. According to the National Institute of Allergy and Infectious Diseases, of the patients that live, about 15 percent will have neurological problems after the infection has cleared up. Another disease of the neurological system that can be caused by complications of chicken pox is meningitis, an inflammation of the fluids around the brain.

Another potential danger of chicken pox is damage to the respiratory system. Sometimes the VZV virus may cause an inflammation of the lungs known as varicella pneumonitis. This is most common in adults, and is especially a risk for pregnant women. Varicella pneumonitis must be watched carefully during pregnancy as it can cause death if it occurs during the last six months of pregnancy.

Chicken Pox and Aspirin: A Deadly Combination

Earlier in this book you were warned about the dangers of mixing aspirin and chicken pox. This deadly combination has killed many people, especially children. Instead of helping, the aspirin may cause severe symptoms, ranging from delirium and severe vomiting to convulsions and, eventually, coma.

Doctors Douglas Reye and George Johnson did research which showed that aspirin could damage many of the body's vital organs. While some victims had mild cases, death was the result for most people who became sick from this interaction. These aspirin complications became known as Reye's syndrome.

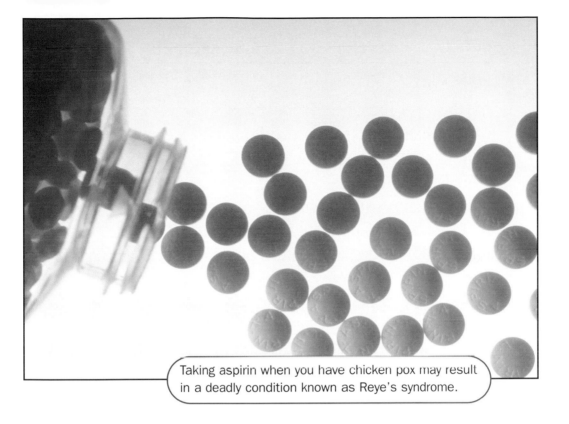

Taking aspirin when you have chicken pox may result in a deadly condition known as Reye's syndrome.

In 1982, the surgeon general issued the warning to avoid taking aspirin to treat chicken pox, the flu, or other respiratory infections. While deaths from Reye's syndrome cannot be entirely blamed on the treatment of viral diseases with aspirin, fewer cases arise now that people are aware of the dangers.

Complications of Shingles

Recovery is expected for most young, healthy people who suffer from shingles. However, for older people with weak immune systems, the pain of shingles can linger for a long time. The main complication associated with shingles is PHN, or post-herepetic neuralgia.

PHN causes the pain of the shingles in the nerve cells to continue for many months or even years after the shingles have otherwise cleared up. Unfortunately, PHN is difficult to treat. It does not respond to antiviral drugs like acyclovir (used to treat shingles in the beginning stages), over-the-counter painkillers, or non-traditional treatments like acupuncture. There are certain antidepressants that dull the pain as it passes through the nerve cells. There are also some topical medicines that can be applied directly to the painful areas.

Remember that the VZV virus affects nerve cells. There are many other possible risks with shingles, including damage to hearing and vision. If the shingles rash appears on the face, it is possible that it can infect the eye or eyelid. If the cornea is affected, temporary or permanent blindness may result. If the virus settles in the facial nerve cells, hearing problems, loss of taste, or facial twitches may result, but only in rare cases.

Chapter Five

Prevention

Until the past decade, there was very little that you could do to prevent anyone from getting chicken pox. If a child in school came down with the pox, the teacher would generally inform classmates' parents, even though at this point the students had already been exposed to the virus and there was nothing that could be done.

The History of the Vaccine

Chicken pox is a part of childhood that most people experience, but scientific research is always searching for ways to make people's lives easier. Scientists wondered why the VZV virus could not be stopped. They began to experiment with possible vaccines for chicken pox.

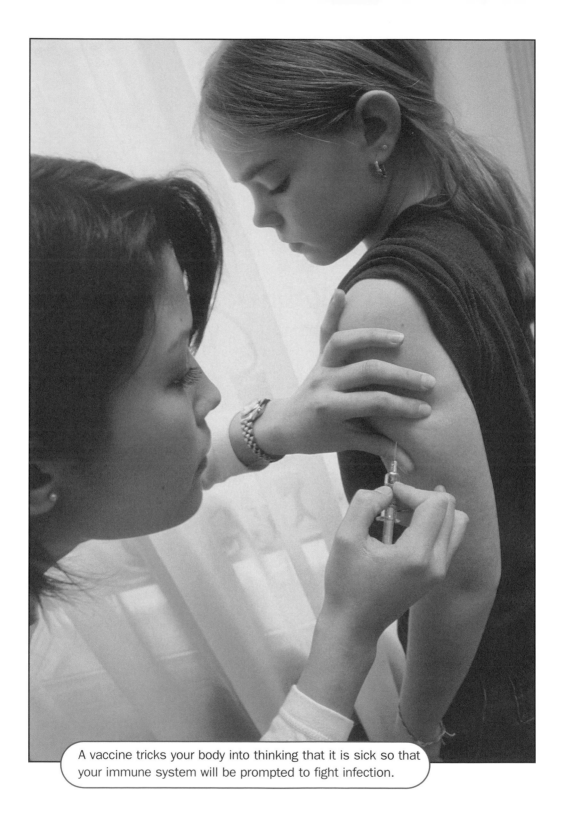

A vaccine tricks your body into thinking that it is sick so that your immune system will be prompted to fight infection.

A vaccine is made up of a form of a particular virus. It is used to prevent disease. When you were a baby, you received vaccinations for diseases like polio and the measles. A vaccine tricks your body into thinking that it is sick. In reaction to this, your immune system will create antibodies to the virus. Then if you ever do come in contact with the virus, the antibodies are already there to fight it.

The first person to search for a chicken pox vaccine was a doctor in Japan. In 1972, he captured a live strain of the VZV virus that causes chicken pox. He called it the Oka strain. Because it was a live virus, he needed to weaken it to the point where it would not make people sick. He worked with this until he believed he had found the right combination to make someone immune to chicken pox. He tried it with children and it worked!

The United States did not start research until 1981 at Merck Laboratories. The researchers at Merck needed to wait to get permission to use the Oka strain for their own testing. In 1982 Merck began testing the Varivax vaccine, which was modeled after the one from Japan. For ten years the researchers administered the vaccine to people to test the results. While some people suffered from mild side effects, the vaccine was effective in developing antibodies for chicken pox. After recieving one dose of the vaccine, about 99 percent of the children were immune to the virus one

Health care workers should be vaccinated against chicken pox.

year later. Adults and teenagers were 97 percent immune after two doses. The vaccine was working! In 1993, Merck took its vaccine to the FDA for approval.

In 1994, the FDA reviewed the vaccine and found that it was safe and that it did work. However, they were still reluctant to approve it for the general public. They had concerns that while children would be immune to the virus, it would still affect adults. Live virus vaccines may actually cause sickness in a person instead of preventing it. The FDA was also unsure if the vaccine would offer lifelong immunity. Despite all of this, in March of 1995, Merck was offered a license to administer the first chicken pox vaccine in the United States.

Is the Vaccine for Everyone?

Now that the vaccine is available, doctors question who should receive it. According to the National Coalition for Adult Immunization, all adults and adolescents who have never had chicken pox before should be immunized. Some people who should receive the vaccine are:

- Health care workers
- Residents and staff at mental health institutions
- Workers and inmates at correctional institutions
- People who live with people with weakened immune systems for whom chicken pox could be very dangerous
- Individuals who travel in foreign countries
- Teachers and day care workers
- College students
- People in the military
- Women who are hoping to become pregnant but who are not already pregnant

The American Academy of Pediatrics approved Varivax in 1995. They suggested that all children from one to one-and-a-half years old should be immunized when they receive their other vaccinations. Children over one-and-a-half years old but younger than twelve should receive one shot of the vaccine. And finally, teenagers and adults who have not had the virus should have two shots of the vaccine about four to eight weeks apart.

Are There Any Health Risks?

There are some people who doctors think should not receive the vaccination. These people include pregnant women, children with weakened immune systems, people who take steroids to help asthma, and people with an allergy to the drug neomycin. With these people there is concern that injecting them with the live vaccine might activate the chicken pox virus in their bodies.

There is debate over the long-term effectiveness of the Varivax vaccine. Many fear that the vaccine might not give lifelong immunity. Because Varivax is new, this outcome is difficult to judge. And as you have learned, what starts as a mild disease in childhood can become very serious if contracted during the adult years. Based on studies performed on the first people vaccinated in Japan, the results seem positive. But it is not possible to know for sure right now.

The remaining health concern is that by receiving a live vaccination you may become sick with the virus. If this does happen, the infection will be mild. You may have some itchiness and a rash, but the recovery will be quick.

Why Get the Immunization?
Despite the arguments that the vaccine may not last, there are many reasons why the chicken pox vaccination is a medical breakthrough. As you have learned, chicken pox is common and rarely dangerous. However, it is an uncomfortable sickness that is best avoided. It costs doctors and patients money for treatment. Not only is it a burden for the person suffering, but because it affects children the most, it often means that parents must stay home from work.

More importantly, the vaccine is important because if you do not get chicken pox as a child you are in danger of catching a more serious form of it as an adult. Although research is still being done, it seems like a good choice for most people, and especially for those who could be in danger of getting very sick if they came down with chicken pox.

Short-Term Prevention

You might be wondering about those people who are high-risk and come in contact with chicken pox before they are vaccinated. There is a way to provide short-term immunity for high-risk individuals, like those discussed in chapter 4. A doctor can administer VZIG, or varicella-zoster immune globulin, to high-risk patients who have been recently exposed to the virus. VZIG is made from the plasma of someone who is immune to chicken pox. Because this blood product contains the antibodies to chicken pox, it offers protection. The protection is only good for three months. But it is helpful for pregnant women, newborns, and people with weakened immune systems who have been exposed to VZV.

What About Shingles?

There is currently no vaccine that will prevent shingles. Doctors hope that as the vaccine prevents people from getting chicken pox, it will also prevent them from getting shingles in the long run. Remember that it is not until you have the VZV virus in your body that you are likely to get shingles. However, there is no proof that this is true. There is concern that, since the live virus hides in the nerve cells, the vaccine itself might eventually lead to shingles.

Research is currently being done to see what happens if people who have already had chicken pox are injected with the varicella vaccine. A small experiment shows that it may lessen the chances of getting shingles later in life. But it is too soon to know this for certain. You can be sure, though, that research will continue in this area.

Glossary

acetaminophen Nonaspirin drug that reduces fever and that can be taken during chicken pox.

acyclovir Antiviral drug that is used to treat chicken pox and shingles.

antibodies Chemical compounds produced by the body that attach to foreign substances to prevent sickness.

antihistamine Drug that reduces swelling or the reaction to a histamine, such as an allergen.

bacteria One-celled organisms that can survive outside of a living cell; sometimes these can be harmful and cause infections in the body.

chicken pox Common childhood disease caused by the varicella-zoster virus that creates an itchy rash on the body.

contagious Infectious; easily transmitted from one person to another.

encephalitis Inflammation of the brain that may be a side effect of chicken pox in rare cases.

herpesvirus Virus family that contains the germs that cause herpes simplex, chicken pox, and mononucleosis.

herpes zoster Shingles virus.

immune system The defenses that your body has to protect you from foreign substances that cause illnesses; made up primarily of white blood cells.

immunity Ability of the body to fight disease.

immunization The vaccination or protection from a particular virus that you receive from a doctor to develop immunity to a disease.

immunocompromised People who have a weakened immune system due to a disease such as AIDS, or from chemotherapy/radiation for cancer.

incubation period Amount of time that it takes for an infection to show symptoms in the body.

infection Presence of a foreign substance or bacteria that can cause harm to the body.

inflammation Swelling or pain located on the body at the point of an infection.

lesion A sore.

live-virus vaccine Vaccine that contains live viruses that have been weakened in a lab; used to produce antibodies for a disease and prevent the actual disease from occurring in the body.

meningitis Inflammation of the fluids that surround the brain.

nervous system Network of cells that send and receive messages in the body; made up of the brain and spinal cord.

nucleic acids Contain the hereditary make-up of an organism; DNA and RNA.

Oka strain Strain of chicken pox used in Japan to make the first live varicella-zoster vaccine.

papule Red, raised bump on the skin that is part of the chicken pox rash.

pneumonitis Inflammation of the lungs; may be a side effect of chicken pox in adults.

post-herpetic neuralgia (PHN) Complication associated with shingles when the pain of the disease never disappears.

pox Swollen sores on the skin that are symptomatic of chicken pox.

pustule Sore on the skin filed with pus.

rash Eruption on the skin, usually consisting of swollen red bumps that cause itchiness and discomfort.

Reye's syndrome Illness associated with taking aspirin when sick with a viral infection; in the past, most common among children.

shingles Disease common among the elderly that is the return of the varicella-zoster virus, this time as a painful rash along nerve endings.

staphylococcus Bacteria that causes skin infections (also known as staph infections).

streptococcus Bacteria that causes skin infections and strep throat.

vaccination Protection against a disease by the introduction of a human-made substance into the bloodstream.

varicella Chicken pox.

varicella-zoster immune globulin (VZIG) Emergency prevention that protects at-risk patients for three months from chicken pox; contains blood of someone who is immune to VZV.

varicella-zoster virus (VZV) The herpesvirus that causes chicken pox and shingles.

virus Simple substance made up of a nucleic acid covered by a protective protein and only able to live and reproduce within another organism's living cells.

Where to Go for Help

In the United States

American Academy of Family Physicians
P.O. Box 11210
Shawnee Mission, KS 66207-1210
(800) 274-2237
Web site: http://www.aafp.org

American Chronic Pain Association
P.O. Box 850
Rocklin, CA 95677
(916) 632-0922
Web site: http://www.theacpa.org

Centers for Disease Control and Prevention (CDC)
Office of Communications
1600 Clifton Road, NE, MSC D25
Atlanta, GA 30333
(404) 423-5679
Web site: http://www.cdc.gov

National Coalition for Adult Immunization
4733 Bethesda Avenue, Suite 750
Bethesda, MD 20814-5228
(301) 656-0003
Web site: http://www.nfid.org/ncai

National Institute of Allergy and Infectious Diseases
Office of Communications
Building 31, Room 7A-50
31 Center Drive, MSC 2520
Bethesda, MD 20892-2520
(301) 496-5717
Web site: http://www.niaid.nih.gov

National Institute of Neurological Disorders
    and Stroke
P. O. Box 5801
Bethesda, MD 20824
(800) 352-9424
Web site: http://www.ninds.nih.gov

VZV Research Foundation
40 East 72nd Street
New York, NY 10021
(800) 472-VIRUS [8478]
Web site: http://www.vzvfoundation.org

In Canada

Canadian Institute for Health Information
90 Eglinton Avenue East, Suite 300
Toronto, ON M4P 2Y3
(416) 481-2002
Web site: http://www.cihi.ca

Canadian Institutes of Health Research (CIHR)
410 Laurier Avenue W., 9th Floor
Address Locator 4209A
(613) 941-2672
Ottawa, ON K1A OW9
Web site: http://www.cihr.ca

In Europe

The World Health Organization
Headquarters Office in Geneva (HQ)
Avenue Appia 20
1211 Geneva 27
Switzerland
(+00 41 22) 791 21 11
Web site: http://www.who.org

Web Sites

Chicken Pox in Pregnancy
http://www.rcog.org.uk/guidelines/chicken_pox.html

Chicken Pox Vaccine
http://www.familydoctor.org/handouts/193.html

KidsHealth by The Nemours Foundation
http://www.kidshealth.org

On Health
http://www.onhealth.webmd.com

For Further Reading

Kotulak, Donna, Dennis Connaughton, and Edward S. Traisman (medical editor). *American Medical Association Complete Guide to Your Children's Health*. New York: Random House, 1999.

Radetsky, Peter. *The Invisible Invaders*. Boston: Little, Brown, 1994.

Schiff, Donald, and Steven P. Shelov (eds.). *Guide to Your Child's Symptoms*. New York: Villard, 1997.

Siegel, Mary-Ellen, and Gray Williams. *Living with Shingles: New Hope for an Old Disease*. New York: M. Evans and Company, Inc., 1998.

Silverstein, Alvin, Virginia Silverstein, and Laura Silverstein Nunn. *Chicken pox and Shingles*. Springfield, NJ: Enslow Publishers, 1998.

Turkington, Carol. *Encyclopedia of Infectious Diseases*. New York: Facts on File, 1998.

Index

Index

N

nerve cells, 10, 13, 26, 27, 30, 35, 44, 52

O

Oka strain, 47
organ transplant, 29, 40

P

post-herpetic neuralgia (PHN), 32, 43

R

rash, 7, 13, 15, 19, 20, 22, 23, 28, 30, 32, 33, 34, 38, 40, 41, 44, 50
Reye's syndrome, 24, 42–44
RNA, 10–11

S

scratching, 20–21
shingles, 10, 13, 14, 26, 27–35, 52
   complications of, 43–44
   contagion of, 32–33
   diagnosis of, 33
   long-term effects of, 41, 44
   possible recurrence of, 34–35
   symptoms of, 30–32
   treatment of, 33–34

staphylococcus bacteria, 41
streptococcus bacteria, 41
stress, 29–30

V

varicella pneumonitis, 42
varicella-zoster immune globulin (VZIG), 51–52
varicella-zoster virus (VZV), 7, 9, 10, 11 13, 14, 15, 19, 23, 26, 27, 28, 33, 32, 34, 37, 38, 41, 42, 44, 45, 47, 52
Varivax vaccine, 47–50
virus, structure of, 10–11

Z

zoster sine herpes, 32
Zovirax (acyclovir), 23

About the Author

Jennifer Plum graduated from Loyola College in Maryland with a degree in nonfiction writing and sociology. She works as a project manager for an educational development house in Baltimore, Maryland, and is a frequent contributor to Discovery Online.

Photo Credits

Cover photo © Francisco Cruz/SuperStock Inc.; p. 2 Lew Lause/SuperStock, Inc.; p. 11 © Oliver Meckes/Gelderblom/PhotoResearchers; p. 12 by Tom Rosenthal/SuperStock Inc.; p. 15 by Richard Heinzen/SuperStock Inc.; pp. 18, 31 by Francisco Cruz/SuperStock Inc.; p. 21 © J. Barabe/Custom Medical Stock Photo; p. 22 Erika Larsen/SuperStock Inc.; p. 25 by Cindy Reiman; p. 29 © John Radcliffe Hospital/Science Photo Library/Photo Researchers; p. 34 © Custom Medical Stock Photo; pp. 39, 46 © SuperStock Inc.; p. 43 © Eric Nelson/Custom Medical Stock Photo; p. 48 © Custom Medical Stock Photo.

Design and Layout

Les Kanturek